American English

Kid's Box

Workbook 2

with Online Resources

Second Edition

Caroline Nixon & Michael Tomlinson

CAMBRIDGE
UNIVERSITY PRESS

CAMBRIDGE
UNIVERSITY PRESS

University Printing House, Cambridge CB2 8BS, United Kingdom

One Liberty Plaza, 20th Floor, New York, NY 10006, USA

477 Williamstown Road, Port Melbourne, VIC 3207, Australia

314–321, 3rd Floor, Plot 3, Splendor Forum, Jasola District Centre, New Delhi – 110025, India

79 Anson Road, #06–04/06, Singapore 079906

Cambridge University Press is part of the University of Cambridge.

It furthers the University's mission by disseminating knowledge in the pursuit of education, learning and research at the highest international levels of excellence.

www.cambridge.org
Information on this title: www.cambridge.org/9781107431348

First published 2008
Second edition 2015
20 19 18 17 16 15 14 13 12 11 10 9

Printed in Malaysia by Vivar Printing

A catalogue record for this publication is available from the British Library

ISBN 978-1-107-43134-8 Workbook with Online Resources 2
ISBN 978-1-107-43127-0 Student's Book 2
ISBN 978-1-107-43161-4 Teacher's Book 2
ISBN 978-1-107-43135-5 Class Audio CDs 2
ISBN 978-1-107-43138-6 Flashcards 2
ISBN 978-1-107-67291-8 Interactive DVD with Teacher's Booklet 2
ISBN 978-1-107-43137-9 Teacher's Resource Book with Online Audio 2
ISBN 978-1-107-43142-3 Presentation Plus 2
ISBN 978-1-107-62900-4 Posters 2
ISBN 978-1-107-69619-8 Tests CD-ROM 1 & 2
ISBN 978-1-107-43144-7 Monty's Alphabet Book

Additional resources for this publication at www.cambridge.org/elt/kidsboxamericanenglish

Kid's Box

American English

Workbook 2

Caroline Nixon & Michael Tomlinson

1  Hi again!

1 🖊 **Write.**

I'm Sally.

I'm Scott.

I'm Suzy.

Hi, I'm Grandma Star. This is my family.

She's __Sally.__ He's _____ _____

I'm Mr. Star.

I'm Mrs. Star.

I'm Grandpa.

_____ _____ _____

2 🖊 **Draw and write.**

What's your name?

_____

How old are you?

_____

4

③  Color the stars.

① ★ ★ ☆ ☆ ☆ ☆ ☆ ☆ ☆ ☆
Color two stars.

② ☆ ☆ ☆ ☆ ☆ ☆ ☆ ☆ ☆ ☆
Color five stars.

③ ☆ ☆ ☆ ☆ ☆ ☆ ☆ ☆ ☆ ☆
Color six stars.

④ ☆ ☆ ☆ ☆ ☆ ☆ ☆ ☆ ☆ ☆
Color one star.

⑤ ☆ ☆ ☆ ☆ ☆ ☆ ☆ ☆ ☆ ☆
Color eight stars.

④ Match and connect.

①	four + one =	7		eight
②	two + one =	5		seven
③	six + one =	8		five
④	eight + one =	6		ten
⑤	five + one =	9		six
⑥	seven + one =	10		three
⑦	nine + one =	3		nine

5 🔊 CD1 7 ✏️ Listen and color.

6 🔊 CD1 8 ✏️ Listen and point. Write the words.

lylaS   Szuy   ctoSt   frou   igteh   sneev

1 This is _Sally._
She's _eight._

2 This is _____
He's _____

3 This is _____
She's _____

Read the question. Listen and write a name or a number. There is one example.

Example

What is the boy's name? ____Dan____

Questions

(1) How old is he? _____

(2) What is his favorite book? _____

(3) Who is next to Dan? _____

(4) How old is she? _____

(5) Which grade is Grace in? _____

8 🔊11 CD1 ✏️ Listen and complete.

1. black
2. g_m_
3. s_y
4. b_g
5. c_t
6. pl_y
7. h_nd
8. sn_k_
9. gr_y
10. _pple

9 🔊12 CD1 ✏️ Listen and write. Match.

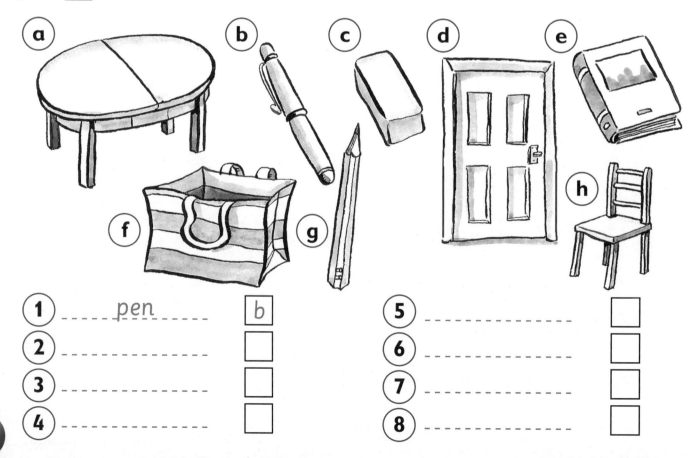

1. _pen_ | b
2. ___ |
3. ___ |
4. ___ |
5. ___ |
6. ___ |
7. ___ |
8. ___ |

My picture dictionary

  Listen and write. Stick.

① _purple_	**②**	**③**
④	**⑤**	**⑥**

My progress

Check (✓) or put an ✗.

I can count to ten. ☐

I can say the colors. ☐

I can say the alphabet. ☐

1 🔍 ✏️ Find and write the words.

desk

```
c u p b o a r d e a t y
l a l o t i n s t r t e
a g a o p e n c i l a f
s r t k c o b o a r d m
s t t c t h a r b a g c
r e r a s e r a f i m h
o f n s h o u b t u o a
o s k e r t l a d e v i
m e n o r t e a c h e r
z h ( d e s k ) r r k p e n
```

2 🔊18 CD1 ✏️ Listen and color.

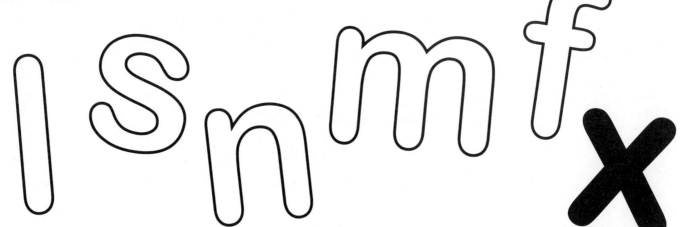

3  Look at the numbers. Write the words.

veleen
11

eleven

niffeet
15

- - - - - - - - -

hiegeetn
18

- - - - - - - - -

ewletv
12

- - - - - - - - -

wytent
20

- - - - - - - - -

reihtnet
13

- - - - - - - - -

4  Read and color.

⑰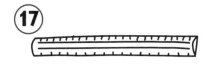

⑲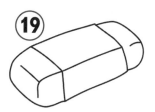

⑯

⑭

Color number twelve brown.
Color number nineteen pink.
Color number fourteen green.
Color number seventeen blue.
Color number sixteen orange.

⑫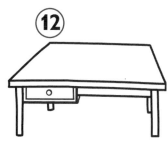

5 ✏️ Write the sentences.

1 (a ruler) (There's) (the table.) (on)

There's a ruler on the table.

2 (the desk.) (There are) (on) (12 pencils)

----

3 (There's) (under) (the chair.) (a backpack)

----

4 (the bookcase.) (16 books) (in) (There are)

----

6 🔍✏️ Look at the picture. Write the answers.

1 How many burgers are there? *There are six.*

2 How many apples are there? _____

3 How many oranges are there? _____

4 How many cupcakes are there? _____

5 How many ice-cream cones are there? _____

6 How many bananas are there? _____

Look and read. Write "yes" or "no."

Example

There are two teachers in the classroom.   _no_

Questions

1. There is a door next to the cupboard. _____
2. There is a board on the wall. _____
3. There are two tables under the board. _____
4. There is a ruler on the bookcase. _____
5. There are two cars under the desk. _____

8 Listen and color red or green.

1. red
2. green
3. tree
4. ten
5. pen
6. read
7. twelve
8. fourteen
9. teacher
10. desk

9 Find the words.

buschoolegrayellowhiteraserruleredesk

How many colors are there? _____

What are they? _____

My picture dictionary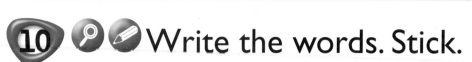

10 🔍✏️ Write the words. Stick.

taechre	baodr	rlure
teacher		
skde	bkoocsae	cpubaord

My progress

Check (✓) or put an ✗.

I can talk about my classroom. ☐

I can say the numbers 11–20. ☐

I can spell. ☐

Now you! **1**  **Ask and answer. Color the graph.**

Which animals do you like?

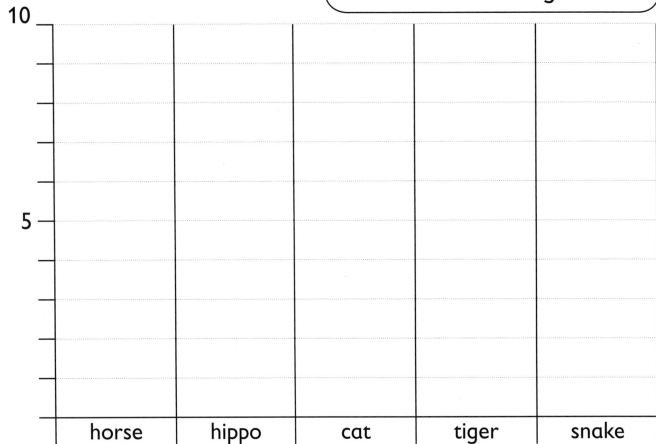

| 10 |
| 5 |
| horse | hippo | cat | tiger | snake |

2 **Answer the questions.**

1. How many children like horses? _ _ _ _ _ _ _ _ _ _
2. How many children like hippos? _ _ _ _ _ _ _ _ _ _
3. How many children like cats? _ _ _ _ _ _ _ _ _ _
4. How many children like tigers? _ _ _ _ _ _ _ _ _ _
5. How many children like snakes? _ _ _ _ _ _ _ _ _ _

16

3 Read and complete.

| come in   Yes, of course.   After you.   Can you spell |

1

— Can we _come in_,
please?
— Yes, come in.

2

— _____
— Thank you.

3

— _____
ruler, please?
— Yes, r-u-l-e-r.

4

— Can you open the
window, please?
— _____

4 Draw a picture of you. Be polite!

Me!

3 Play time!

1 🔍 ✏️ **Read. Circle the "toy" words. Write.**

k i t e

_ _ _ _ _ _ _ _   _ _ _ _ _

_ _ _ _ _

Suzy has a (kite). Scott has a robot.
Robert has a train. Eva has a car.
Sally has a computer game. Alex
has a big yellow watch.

_ _ _ _   _ _ _ _ _ _

2 🔊 33 CD1 ✏️ **Listen and check (✔) the box.**

(3) ✏️ Complete the sentences and color the pictures.

(1) <u>This</u> is a red plane.

(2) <u>These</u> are purple watches.

(3) _____ are blue trucks.

(4) _____ is a brown doll.

(5) _____ are green balls.

(6) _____ are gray robots.

(7) _____ are yellow cameras.

(8) _____ are blue kites.

(4) ✏️ Match. Write the words.

k	*kitchen*	*kite*	~~itchen~~	obot
c			amera	ain
r			uler	~~ite~~
d			oll	ane
tr			uck	og
pl			ease	ake

5 🔊38 CD1 ✏️ Listen and color. Then answer.

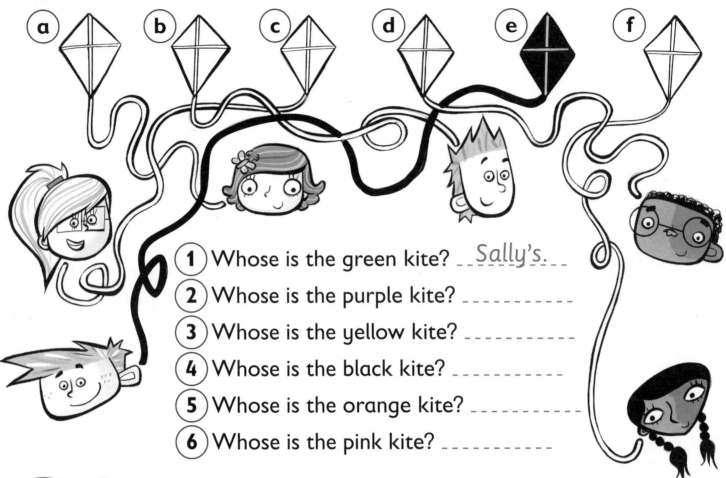

(a) (b) (c) (d) (e) (f)

1 Whose is the green kite? _Sally's._
2 Whose is the purple kite? _ _ _ _ _ _ _ _ _ _
3 Whose is the yellow kite? _ _ _ _ _ _ _ _ _ _
4 Whose is the black kite? _ _ _ _ _ _ _ _ _ _
5 Whose is the orange kite? _ _ _ _ _ _ _ _ _ _
6 Whose is the pink kite? _ _ _ _ _ _ _ _ _ _

6 ✏️ Write the questions.

1 _Whose is the truck?_ _ _ _ _ _ _ _ _ _   It's Bill's.
2 _   It's Lucy's.
3 _   It's Ben's.
4 _   It's Kim's.
5 _   It's Tony's.

7 Look and read. Put a ✓ or an ✗ in the box. There is one example.

Example

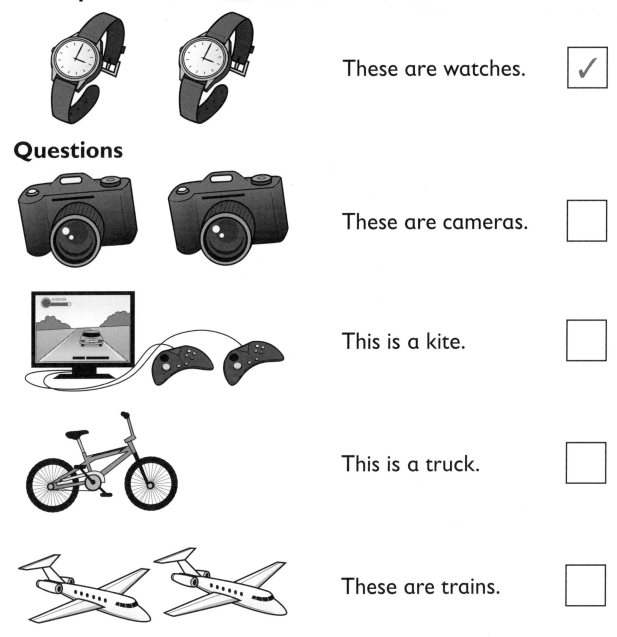

These are watches. ✓

Questions

These are cameras. ☐

This is a kite. ☐

This is a truck. ☐

These are trains. ☐

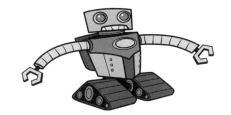

This is a robot. ☐

8 🎵 42 CD1 ✏️ Listen and write the words.

(1) ~~fish~~   (2) ~~kite~~   (3) pink   (4) five   (5) my

(6) swim   (7) bike   (8) big   (9) fly   (10) sit

fish
_____
_____
_____
_____

kite
_____
_____
_____
_____

9 🎵 43 CD1 ✏️ Listen and connect the dots.

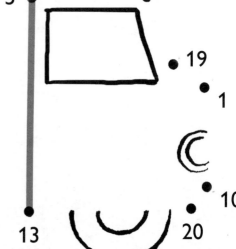

14

6 •

•3

5 •2

17 •

•19

•1

8 •

11 •

13 •20

•10

What is it?   It's a _____ .

22

My picture dictionary

10 CD1 45 ✏ Listen and stick. Write the words.

① _ _ kite _ _

② _ _ _ _ _ _

③ _ _ _ _ _ _

④ _ _ _ _ _ _

⑤ _ _ _ _ _ _

⑥ _ _ _ _ _ _

My progress

Check (✓) or put an ✗.

I can talk about my favorite toy. ☐

I can write "toy" words. ☐

4 At home

1 🎧48 CD1 ✏️ Listen and draw lines.

2 ✏️ Write the words.

Across →

② ③

⑦ ⑧ ⑨

Down ↓

① ④ ⑥

③ ⑤

		¹		
²l	a	m	p	

3 _____ 4 _____

5 _____ 6 _____

7 _____ 8 _____

9 _____

3 Read and write the number. Draw.

sixteen = _16_ → m	twelve = _____ → c
fourteen = _____ → l	fifteen = _____ → a
seventeen = _____ → r	thirteen = _____ → i
eighteen = _____ → o	nineteen = _____ → u
twenty = _____ → p	eleven = _____ → h

①

m					
16	13	17	17	18	17

②

14	15	16	20

③

12	18	19	12	11

Me!

4 Read and write the words.

phone ~~mirror~~ couch rug armchair

① You can see your face in it. _mirror_

② Four children can sit on it. _____

③ It's small. It has numbers on it, and you can talk to
your friends on it. _____

④ One child can sit on it. _____

⑤ You can place it on the floor in your bedroom,
and it can have a lot of colors. _____

5 ✏️ Write "yours" or "mine."

6 🔊53 CD1 ✏️ Listen and color.

7 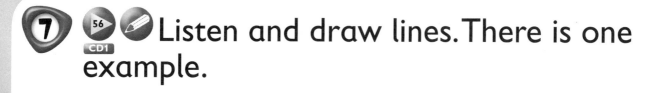 Listen and draw lines. There is one example.

  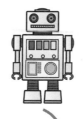 

27

8 🔊58 CD1 ✏️ Listen and write the words.

(1) ~~boat~~ (2) ~~box~~ (3) doll (4) phone (5) clock

(6) clothes (7) yell<u>ow</u> (8) ro<u>bo</u>t (9) socks (10) old

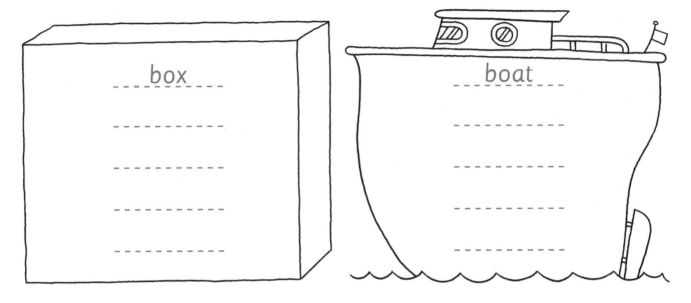

box

boat

9 ✏️ Write the words.

This	~~That~~	These	Those	These	That

(1) That is a couch.

(2) _____ is a phone.

(3) _____ are armchairs.

(4) _____ is a clock.

(5) _____ are rugs.

(6) _____ are beds.

28

My picture dictionary

10  Complete the words. Stick.

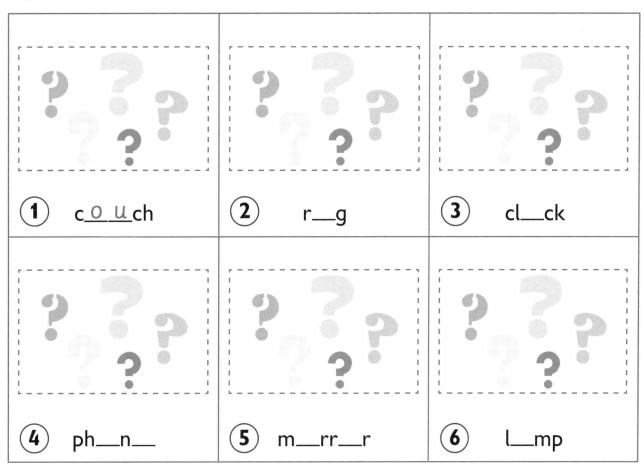

① c _o_ _u_ ch

② r__g

③ cl__ck

④ ph__n__

⑤ m__rr__r

⑥ l__mp

My progress

Check (✓) or put an ✗.

I can talk about my house. ☐

I can say what's mine. ☐

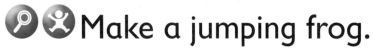
Now you! **1** 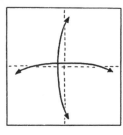Make a jumping frog.

 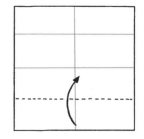 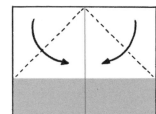 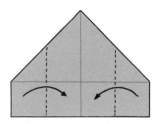

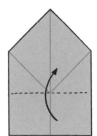 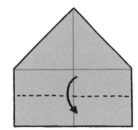 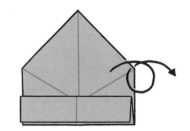 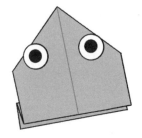

2 Look and write.

| ~~robot~~ couch cupboard kite phone lamp |

1

robot

2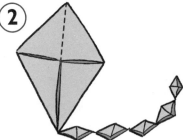

_____

3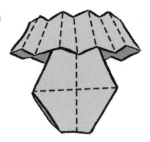

_____

4

_____

5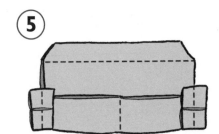

_____

6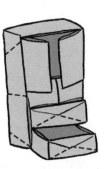

_____

3 🔍✏️ Look, read, and match.

①    ②   ③   ④

a an old
T-shirt

b an old
sock

c old paper

d a plastic
bottle

4 ✏️ You have four boxes, two socks, a
T-shirt, and five pencils. Draw a robot.

Review

1 2 3 4

1 ✏️ Match the color.

7 gray	nine	**8** yellow	three	**5** pink
6 blue	ten	two	**10** orange	four
five	**3** purple	**9** green	eight	**1** brown
2 red	seven	six	**4** black	one

2 🔊 5 CD2 ✏️ Listen and write the number.

13

3 Write the questions. Answer the questions.

	a	b	c	d	e	f
1	what	trucks	dirty	how	big	bed
2	shoes	toy	clean	small	balls	whose
3	is	small	camera	many	are	chair
4	there	under	where	on	the	or

1 4c 3e 4e 1b

Where are the trucks _____ ?

_____ .

2 2f 2b 3a 4d 4e 1f

_____ ?

_____ .

3 3e 4e 2a 2c 4f 1c

_____ ?

_____ .

4 1d 3d 1b 3e 4a

_____ ?

_____ .

5 4c 3a 4e 3c

_____ ?

_____ .

6 1a 3a 4d 4e 3f

_____ ?

_____ .

5 Meet my family

1 🔍✏️ Read and write the names.

This is Robert and his family. He's with his brother Sam, his sister May, and his cousin Frank. Robert's brother has a big nose. Robert has small eyes. Robert's cousin is young. He's a baby. Robert's sister has long hair.

2 ✏️ Write the words.

~~couch~~   ~~mommy~~   ~~plane~~   ~~bookcase~~   teacher   grandma   baby
kite   desk   truck   grandpa   playground   cousin   rug   robot
board   mirror   boat   lamp   daddy   bed   ruler   doll   phone

In the house
couch

Family
mommy

Toys
plane

In the school
bookcase

③ 🔍 ✏️ Read. Write the name. Color.

⑫ ⑦ ㉟ ㊶

------------------------- ------------------------- ------------------------- -------------------------

Hi. This is my family. My mommy has long purple hair, small green ears, and five yellow teeth. Her name's Trudy. My daddy's name's Tom. He has short red hair and a dirty green nose. He has eight brown teeth. My brother Tony has long brown hair, big red eyes, and one white tooth. My sister's name is Tricia. She's very clean! She has big ears, short blue hair, orange eyes, and six green teeth.

④ 🔍 ✏️ Write the words.

(bbya)   (afntharedrg)   (anthmoredrg)   (oremth)

(sstire)   (fthrea)   (ddyda)   (csinou)   (rthbore)   (ymmmo)

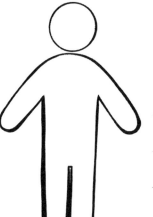

baby _____

_____

_____

_____

baby _____

_____

_____

_____

5  **Listen and write the number.**

6 🔍✏️ **Look at the pictures and write the letters.**

1 – What are you doing, Mom? [c]

– I'm making a cake. [d]

2 – Whose kite are you flying, Scott? [ ]

– I'm flying your kite, Suzy. [ ]

3 – What are you eating, Dad? [ ]

– I'm eating chocolate ice cream. [ ]

4 – Whose shoes are you cleaning, Grandpa? [ ]

– I'm cleaning Scott's shoes. [ ]

5 – Which word are you spelling, Sally? [ ]

– I'm spelling "beautiful." [ ]

6 – What are you drawing, Grandma? [ ]

– I'm drawing Sally. [ ]

7 **13** CD2 Listen and check (✓) the box.
There is one example.

Example

What is Dan doing?

Questions

1 Which is Anna?

2 What's Sue doing?

3 What's Grandpa doing?

4 What's Sam drawing?

8 **15** CD2 Listen and write.

1 b<u>u</u>s

2 sh___

3 tr_ck

4 S___

5 s_n

6 r_ler

7 bl___

8 r_n

9 j_mp

9 Write the letters.

a	He's kicking	his car.	
b	They're cleaning	in her bed.	
c	He's driving	a ball.	a
d	She's sleeping	books.	
e	We're singing	a song.	
f	I'm playing	the guitar.	
g	They're reading	their rooms.	

My picture dictionary

  Listen and write. Stick.

? ? ? ? ?	? ? ? ? ?	? ? ? ? ?
① _grandma_	② _ _ _ _ _	③ _ _ _ _ _
? ? ? ? ?	? ? ? ? ?	? ? ? ? ?
④ _ _ _ _ _	⑤ _ _ _ _ _	⑥ _ _ _ _ _

My progress

Check (✓) or put an ✗.

I can talk about my family. ☐

I can talk about actions. ☐

1 🔍 ✏️ Read the lists and find the food.

Draw lines with a pencil. Draw lines with a pen.

a Shopping list

- oranges
- bread
- rice
- bananas
- apples
- milk
- ice cream
- burgers
- apple juice
- eggs
- water

b Shopping list

- potatoes
- rice
- bread
- carrots
- fish
- orange juice
- fries
- chicken
- lemons
- meat

Start

Start

Finish

Finish

2  **Find and color.**

Color the pears green.
Color the carrots orange.
Color the tomatoes red.

Color the chicken brown.
Color the meat red.
Color the lemons yellow.

3 **Draw and write about your favorite food. Ask and answer.**

Me!

What's your favorite food for dinner?

It's chicken and fries.

My favorite food is

4 **25** CD2 ✏️ Listen and check (✓) or put an ✗.

① ✗

②

③

④

5 🔍 ✏️ Read and write the numbers.

Here you are. ☐

Can I have some juice, please? 1

Orange juice, please. ☐

Which juice – orange juice or apple juice? ☐

Which fruit – a banana, a pear, or an apple? ☐

Here you are. ☐

Can I have some fruit, please? ☐

A pear, please. ☐

6 🔍✏️ Read and choose a word from the box. Write the word next to numbers 1–5. There is one example.

A kitchen

I am in a ___house___ . Anna and her (1) _____

have breakfast in me. On the table, there are apples and

(2) _____ . Anna is drinking (3) _____ and eating a

(4) _____ . Anna's brother is very happy today. He is eating

his favorite food. It is a small, white (5) _____ with bread.

What am I? I am a kitchen.

oranges   brother   chairs   egg

teacher   ~~house~~   banana   milk

7   Listen and write the words.

| teacher | chair | watch | ~~children~~ | chicken | kitchen | lunch | chocolate |

1 children

2

3

4

5

6

7

8

Write the words and the letters.

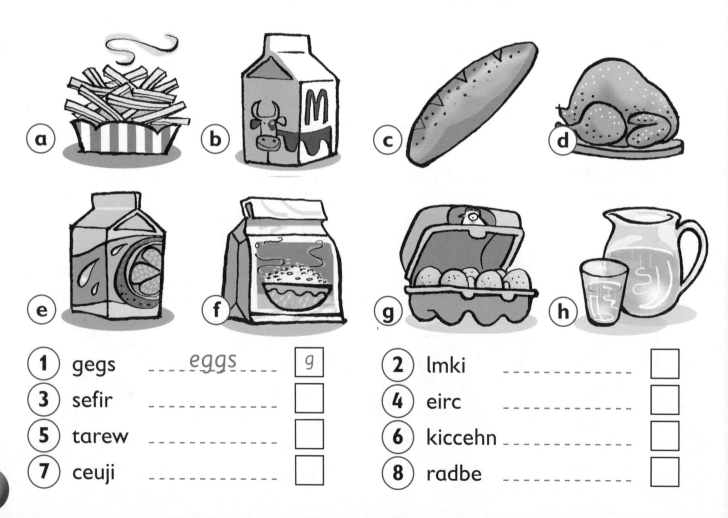

1 gegs _____ eggs _____ | g |

2 lmki _____ | |

3 sefir _____ | |

4 eirc _____ | |

5 tarew _____ | |

6 kiccehn _____ | |

7 ceuji _____ | |

8 radbe _____ | |

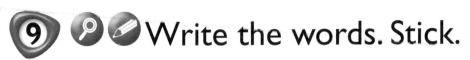

My picture dictionary

9 🔍 ✏️ Write the words. Stick.

ckinehc	**gegs**	**rifes**
chicken	------	------
lkmi	**rcie**	**dearb**
------	------	------

My progress

Check (✔) or put an ✗.

I can talk about my favorite food. ☐

I can talk about breakfast, lunch, ☐ and dinner.

I can ask and answer questions ☐ about food.

1 Read and match.

| milk | meat | eggs | lemons | potatoes | carrots |

Now you! 2 Write the words.

apples   potatoes   milk   carrots   eggs   lemons
meat   chicken   oranges   rice   pears   tomatoes

From animals …   From plants …   From trees …

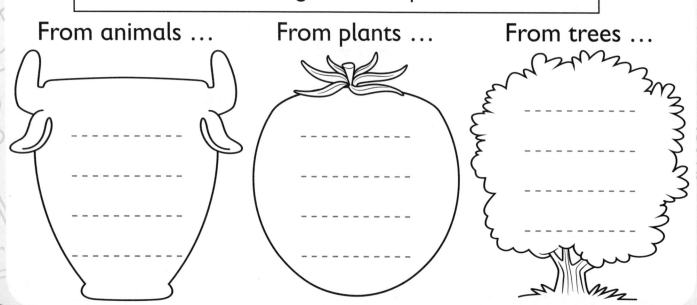

3 Draw your favorite food.

milk   bread   eggs   juice   chicken   rice   water
fish   carrots   apples   meat   potatoes   bananas   oranges

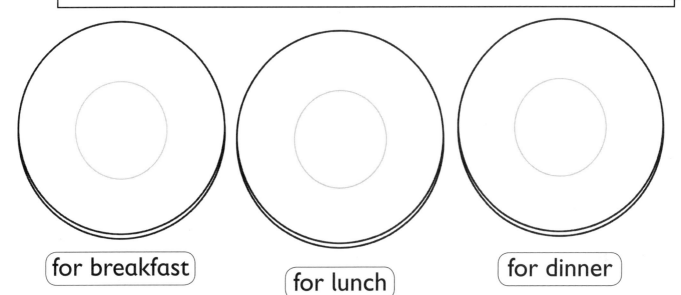

for breakfast

for lunch

for dinner

4 Now tell your partner.
Draw your friend's food.

What's your favorite food for breakfast?

I like oranges and apples.

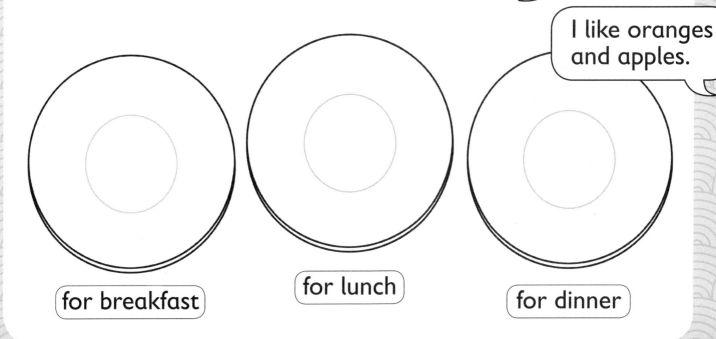

for breakfast

for lunch

for dinner

7 On the farm

1 🔍✏️ Find and write the words.

```
w a l e r s d s p i
s h e e p t u p l d
e d m e y k c i r a
p m i u s a k d b y
t h c h i c k e n a
e w t o g o y r o b
c a s r z w i l s i
h f i s h e t r h r
a r t e l i z a r d
m o u s e f r e n d
s g o a t r f r e v
```

horse

_____ _____ _____ _____

_____ _____ _____ _____

2 🔍✏️ Read. Draw and write the words.

~~snakes~~ ~~crocodiles~~ fish lizards birds giraffes tigers monkeys

This is the Star Zoo. The birds are next to the snakes. The fish are under the birds. The lizards are between the fish and the monkeys. The yellow and brown animals next to the monkeys are giraffes. The big orange and black cats under the crocodiles are tigers.

snakes

crocodiles

3 ✏️ Draw lines.

💬✏️ Now ask your friend and draw lines.

Where is the cow?　　　It's in the cupboard.

4 [38] [CD2] Write the words. Listen and check.

| love | I | So | do | I | love | lizards | don't |

1
a I _love_ spiders.

b So do _____ .

2
c _____ love fish.

d _____ do I.

3
e I love _____ .

f So _____ I.

4
g I _____ goats.

h I _____ .

5 Draw your favorite animal.
Ask your friend.

What's your favorite animal?

Me!

I love _____ .

6 **40** **CD2** Listen and color. There is one example.

7   Listen and write.

(1)
sp ider

(2)
__ar

(3)
__ake

(4)
__im

(5)
__irt

(6)
__ow

(7)
__orts

(8)
____ool

8 Write the "animal" words.

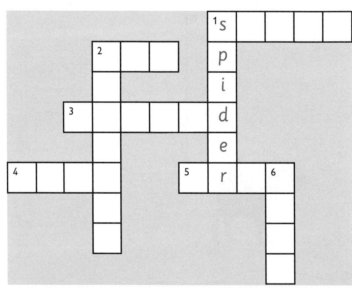

Down

(1) This is small and black, and it has eight legs.
(2) We get eggs from this farm bird.
(6) This farm animal can eat clothes.

Across

(1) This farm animal has a short tail and a lot of white hair.
(2) We get milk from this big farm animal.
(3) This green or brown animal has four short legs, a long body, and a long thin tail.
(4) This bird has orange feet. It can swim.
(5) This small green animal has big feet and long legs. It can swim and jump.

My picture dictionary

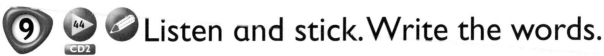 Listen and stick. Write the words.

① spider

② ____

③ ____

④ ____

⑤ ____

⑥ ____

My progress

Check (✓) or put an ✗.

I can write "animal" words. ☐

I can talk about things I love. ☐

8 My town

1 🔍✏️ Look and read. Check (✓) or put an ✗ in the box.

1 This is an apartment. **✗**

2 This is a store. ☐

3 This is a hospital. ☐

4 This is a street. ☐

5 This is a park. ☐

6 This is a café. ☐

2 ✏️ Circle the different word.

1 car	truck	bus	(store)
2 apartment	town	goat	street
3 bike	café	hospital	school
4 kitchen	bedroom	bathroom	park
5 store	cupboard	armchair	couch
6 street	park	school	bedroom
7 frog	hospital	café	apartment
8 door	town	window	floor

3 🔍✏️ **Spot the differences.**

① In A *there's one car*   , but in B *there are two cars*   .
② In A _____ , but in B _____ .
③ In A _____ , but in B _____ .
④ In A _____ , but in B _____ .
⑤ In A _____ , but in B _____ .
⑥ In A _____ , but in B _____ .

4 ✏️ **Write the words.**

~~ball~~ ~~pear~~ ~~chair~~ ~~dog~~ coconut armchair table bike apple
computer game lizard pineapple cat train car lemon
truck fish mouse mirror clock orange bird cupboard

FRED'S FRUIT

pear
_____
_____
_____
_____
_____

TED'S TOYS

ball
_____
_____
_____
_____
_____

Pete's Pets

dog
_____
_____
_____
_____
_____

Phil's Furniture

chair
_____
_____
_____
_____
_____

5  Listen and color the stars.

6 Read and write the names.

You're Tom. You're sitting in front of Jill.
You're Ann. You're sitting between Tom and Nick.
You're Bill. You're sitting behind Nick.
You're Sue. You're sitting between Jill and Bill.

7 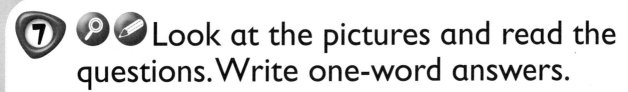 Look at the pictures and read the questions. Write one-word answers.

Example

Where are the children?   in front of a ....*café*.......

Questions

① What color is the dog?   - - - - - - - - - - - - - - - - - -

② How many children are there?   - - - - - - - - - - - - - - - - - -

③ Who is eating the
ice-cream cone?   the - - - - - - - - - - - - - - - - -

④ Where is the dog?   - - - - - - - - - - - - - - - - - the
                                  table and the chair

⑤ What is the dog doing?   it is - - - - - - - - - - - - - - - -

52 **CD2** **Listen and write the words.**

| cow | mouse | ~~brown~~ | house | mouth | down | couch | town |

(1)

(2)

(3)

(4)

brown _____ _____ _____ _____

(5)

(6)

(7)

(8)

sit _____ _____ _____ _____

 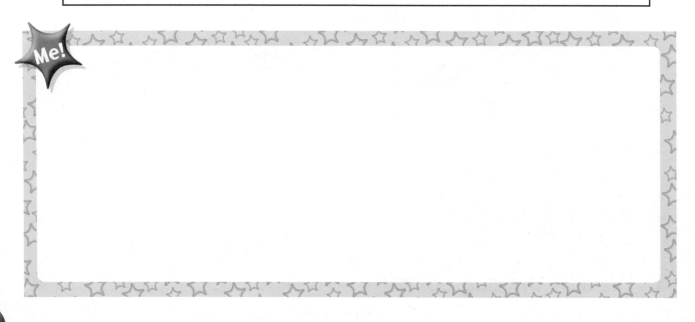

Draw a town. Use these words.

| pet store | café | bookstore | hospital | apartment | park |

Me!

My picture dictionary

10  Complete the words. Stick.

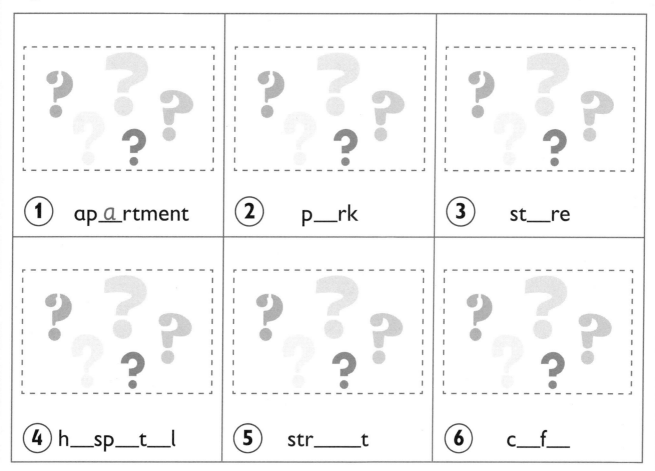

① ap _a_ rtment

② p__rk

③ st__re

④ h__sp__t__l

⑤ str____t

⑥ c__f__

My progress

Check (✓) or put an ✗.

I can talk about the town. ☐

I can write about the town. ☐

1 Listen and say the animal.

a cat　a bird　a frog　an elephant　a sheep　a cow

It's a bird.　　They're cats.

Now you! **2**  Make a guitar.

3 Read and circle.

1. There's a **red** / **green** traffic light. You can cross the road.

2. Don't play soccer **on the road** / **at the park**.

3. The sign says: **Don't walk** / **Walk** on the grass.

4. Put your **trash** / **books** in the trash can.

5. Don't cross the road. The traffic light is **green** / **red**.

4  Look and write "can" or "can't."

1. I __can__ put my trash here.

2. I _____ sit here.

3. I _____ cross the road here.

4. I _____ play here.

Review

5 6 7 8

 Find and write the words.

"food" words	t g d r t y z x d j u	"family" words
milk	b r e a k f a s t u w	brother
_____	r a a m o m m y f i g	_____
_____	o n w n m c j x r c h	_____
_____	t d a d d y o s i e e	_____
_____	h m s l o i i i e k d	_____
_____	e o p a b h k s s s i	_____
_____	r t m (m i l k) t s m n	_____
_____	o h c k s o i e m g n	
	o e g g s j u r x k e	
	g r a n d f a t h e r	

 Listen and write the number.

1

3   Read and draw lines.

The baby is behind the door.
The mother is between the bed and the desk.
The clock is on the bookcase, between the books.
The lamp is on the desk.
The goat is on the desk, in front of the lamp.
There's a spider under the bed.

4 🔊7 CD3 ✏️ Listen and complete. Chant.

Whose Which ~~Who~~ What How many Where who How old What

(1) __Who__ is that?
That's my brother, Paul.

(2) _____'s he doing?
He's catching a ball.

(3) _____ ball is it?
It's my cousin Nick's.

(4) _____ is he?
He's very young.
He's only six.

(5) _____ is he now?
He's in the hallway.

(6) _____'s he doing?
He's throwing his ball.

(7) _____ balls do you have?
I don't know!
We have a lot.

(8) _____ one's your favorite – red or blue?
I don't know!

(9) And _____ are you?

63

9 Our clothes

1  Listen and connect the dots.

2 Follow the "clothes" words.

watch	shoes	glasses	lizard	cake
meat	frog	socks	burger	sheep
hat	T-shirt	jeans	carrots	goat
pants	ice cream	cow	bread	spider
dress	skirt	jacket	shirt	purse

How many clothes are there? _____

Write the "animal" words. _____

Write the "food" words. _____

3 ✏️ Write the words and color the picture.

a	b	c	d	e	f	g	h	i	j	k	l	m
☆	■	○	▭	◆	◨	●	★	◈	△	▼	⌣	◐

n	o	p	q	r	s	t	u	v	w	x	y	z
▲	☆	◤	◇	▲	⌣	▽	□	▬	⌣	▽	▭	◸

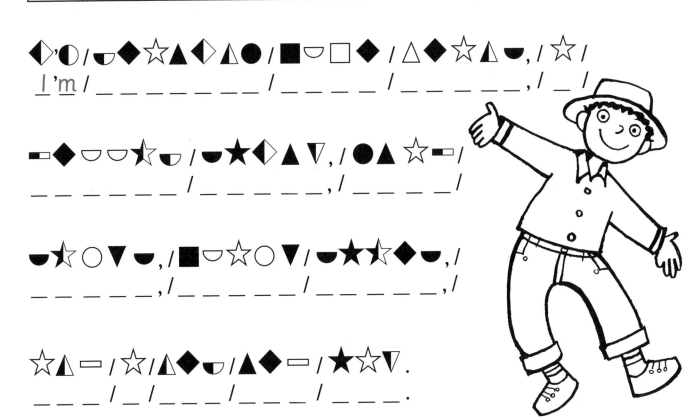

I'm / _ _ _ _ _ _ _ / _ _ _ _ _ _ / _ _ _ _ _ , / _ /

_ _ _ _ _ _ _ / _ _ _ _ _ , / _ _ _ _ /

_ _ _ _ _ , / _ _ _ _ _ _ / _ _ _ _ _ , /

_ _ _ / _ / _ _ _ / _ _ _ / _ _ _ .

4 ✏️ Describe your clothes.

Me!

I'm wearing _____

_____

_____

_____

5 🔍✏️ Look and write.

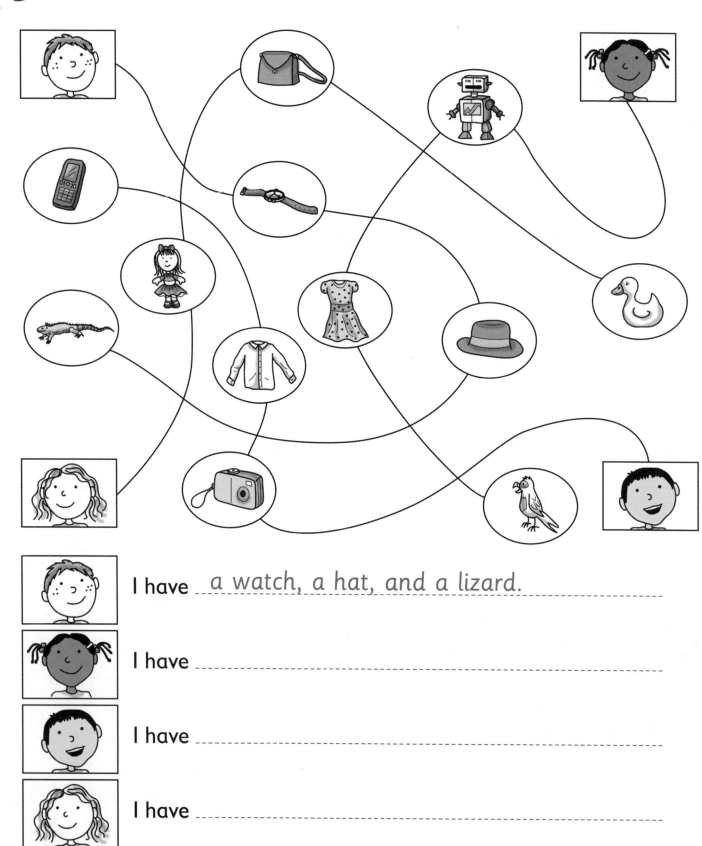

I have a watch, a hat, and a lizard. ------------------------------

I have ---

I have ---

I have ---

6 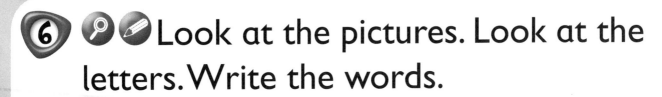 Look at the pictures. Look at the letters. Write the words.

Example

<u>T-s h i r t</u>

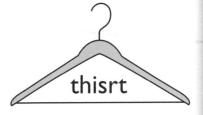
thisrt

Questions

1

_ _ _

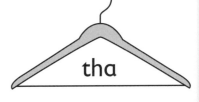
tha

2

_ _ _ _ _

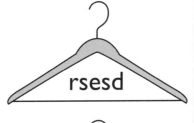
rsesd

3

_ _ _ _ _ _

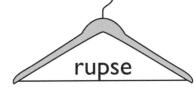
rupse

4

_ _ _ _ _

snjae

5

_ _ _ _ _ _ _

ssslega

7  Listen and write.

1. s**h**eep
2. __ __oe
3. _even
4. sock_
5. __ __irt
6. de_k
7. fi__ __
8. dre__ __
9. _leep
10. _tore

8 Cross out five objects. Ask your friend.

Do you have a hat?

Yes, I do.

hat	✓	lemon	
purse		cow	
shoe		sheep	
glasses		monster	
frog		tomato	

My picture dictionary

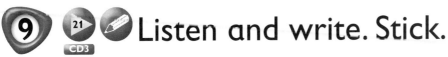 **9** **21** CD3 Listen and write. Stick.

1. purse

2.

3.

4.

5.

6.

My progress

Check (✓) or put an X.

I can talk about my clothes. ☐

I can talk about things I have. ☐

69

10 Our hobbies

1 ✏️ Write the words and the numbers.

① ② ③ ④ ⑤ ⑥

ptingain ___painting___ 4   itagur _____ ☐

btonadmin _____ ☐   iPgn-ongP _____ ☐

ildef hokeyc _____ ☐   ebbasall _____ ☐

2 🔊24 CD3 ✏️ Listen and color.

③ ✏ Write the words.

Down ↓ **Across →**

④ ✏ Complete the sentences.

③ → They're _swimming._

④ ↓ She's _____

⑥ → She's _____

⑥ ↓ They're _____ _____

⑨ → He's _____

⑩ → They're _____ _____

5 🔊 27 CD3 ✏️ Listen and check (✓) or put an **X**.

1 ⓐ ✓   ⓑ ☐   ⓒ ☐

2 ⓐ ☐   ⓑ ☐   ⓒ ☐

3 ⓐ ☐   ⓑ ☐   ⓒ ☐

4 ⓐ ☐   ⓑ ☐   ⓒ ☐

6 ✏️ Draw and write about you.

My name's _____ .

I'm _____ years old.

My hair is _____ .

My eyes are _____ .

My favorite toy is _____ .

I like _____ .

I don't like _____ .

I love _____ .

My favorite hobby is _____ .

Me!

7 🔍✏️ Look and read. Write "yes" or "no."

Example

Two girls are playing field hockey.   _no_

Questions

1 A boy is wearing a black T-shirt.   _____

2 Two boys are playing Ping-Pong.   _____

3 A tall girl is playing basketball.   _____

4 The boy under the tree is playing the guitar.   _____

5 A girl in a white skirt is playing badminton.   _____

8 🎵 31 CD3 ✏️ **Listen and match.**

① A lo**ng** dog. ___c___
② The boy's eati**ng**. _____
③ She's si**ng**ing a so**ng**. _____
④ The ki**ng**'s readi**ng**. _____
⑤ She's painti**ng**. _____

ⓐ

ⓑ

ⓒ

ⓓ

ⓔ

9 🔍 ✏️ **Read. Write the words.**

Hi. I'm Tom. Now, I'm at

_____school_____ . I'm playing

_____ . I'm wearing

a red and white _____

and long blue _____ .

I like playing sports.

For lunch today, I have

some _____ and an

_____ . I like having

lunch at school.

74

My picture dictionary

10   Write the words. Stick.

bdanimtno	ginP-gonP	bsaeblal
badminton		
bakstebllo	pniatngi	delfi oeyckh

My progress

Check (✓) or put an ✗.

I can write "sport" and "hobby" words. ☐

I can talk about my likes. ☐

Now you! 1 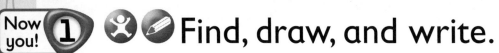 Find, draw, and write.

Things we wear   Red things

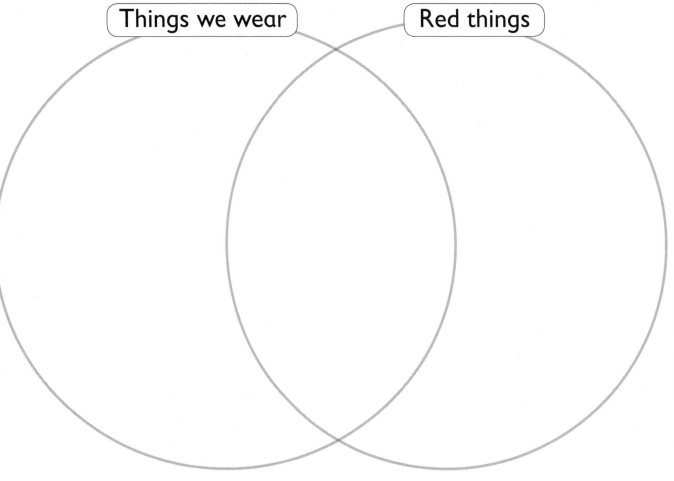

2 Write about your Venn diagram.

There are _____ red things.

There are _____ things we wear.

There are _____ red things we wear.

3 Look and check (✓) or put an ✗.

You can run with the ball.

Right rule? ☐

Wrong rule? ☐

You can throw the ball.

Right rule? ☐

Wrong rule? ☐

You can kick the ball.

Right rule? ☐

Wrong rule? ☐

You can hit the ball with your hands.

Right rule? ☐

Wrong rule? ☐

4 Listen and say the sport.

It's basketball.

77

1 ✏️ Write the letters and the words.

u

__ __ u __ __ __ __ __ __

__ __ __ __ __ __ __ __ __

2 🔍✏️ Circle the different words.

1 tree	yard	flower	(car)
2 shoe	camera	robot	kite
3 sausage	armchair	chicken	fries
4 lemonade	orange	milk	water
5 badminton	basketball	soccer	bus
6 café	desk	hospital	school
7 cupboard	bed	couch	kitchen
8 kitchen	hallway	bathroom	mirror

3   Listen and draw.

4 Write the words.

| me | you | her | it | us | ~~them~~ |

1

Look at ___them___ .

2

Can I play with _____ ?

3

Smile at _____ .

4

Take a picture of _____ .

5

Come and play with _____ .

6

Take a picture of _____ .

5 ✏️ Write the sentences.

① (fries?) (some) (Would) (like) (you)

Would you like some fries?

② (some) (please.) (cake,) (like) (I'd)

_____

③ (Would) (like) (you) (to play) (us?) (with)

_____

④ (to play) (I'd) (Ping-Pong.) (like)

_____

6 🔍✏️ Read and write the information.

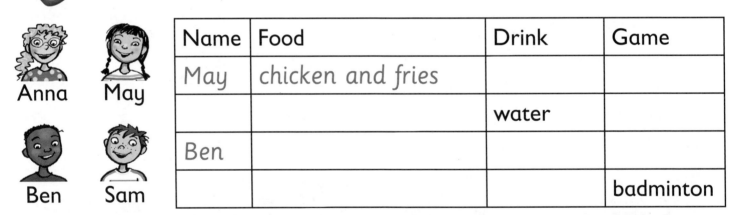

Anna   May

Ben   Sam

Name	Food	Drink	Game
May	chicken and fries		
		water	
Ben			
			badminton

It's Anna's birthday, and she's having lunch with her three friends, May, Ben, and Sam.

① May would like some chicken and fries, and she'd like some orange juice.

② Ben would like some burgers and potatoes.

③ One boy would like some sausages and tomatoes, and he'd like some water.

④ Two children would like some lemonade.

⑤ The two boys would like to play field hockey, and the two girls would like to play badminton.

⑥ One girl would like some carrots and rice. It's her birthday today.

7 Listen and draw lines. There is one example.

  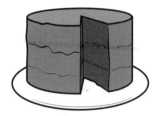

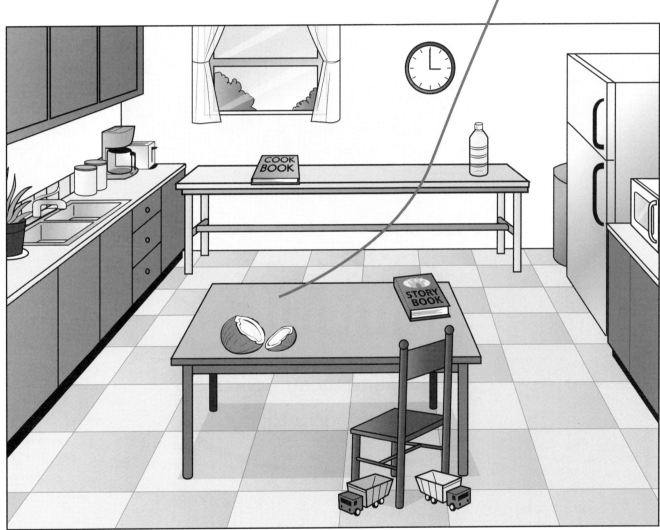

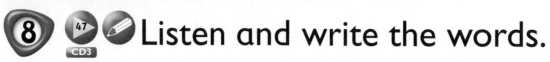

8 🔊 47 CD3 ✏️ **Listen and write the words.**

| sk<u>ir</u>t | b<u>ir</u>d | ~~purple~~ | th<u>ir</u>teen | b<u>ur</u>ger | sh<u>ir</u>t | g<u>ir</u>l | b<u>ir</u>thday |

①

purple

②

③

④

⑤

⑥

⑦

⑧

9 🔍 ✏️ **Look at the letters. Write words.**

Happy birthday, Scott.
It's your party today!

shirt

My picture dictionary

  Listen and stick. Write the words.

① ___cake___

② _____

③ _____

④ _____

⑤ _____

⑥ _____

My progress

Check (✓) or put an ✗.

I can ask for food and drink. ☐

I can talk about party food. ☐

1 🔊 CD4 🔍 Listen and check (✓). Find the words.

1. ocean ✓ open ☐
2. song ☐ sun ☐
3. sand ☐ hand ☐
4. shell ☐ she ☐
5. mountain ☐ mouth ☐
6. three ☐ tree ☐
7. floors ☐ flowers ☐
8. bird ☐ big ☐
9. animals ☐ apples ☐
10. phone ☐ fish ☐
11. vacation ☐ train ☐

a	s	m	o	b	s	a	n	r
f	h	o	b	i	t	a	y	h
l	e	u	t	r	e	n	g	m
o	l	n	i	d	f	i	s	h
w	l	t	s	u	n	m	e	t
e	m	a	o	c	e	a	n	r
r	u	i	h	k	h	l	o	e
s	a	n	d	a	r	s	t	e
b	v	a	c	a	t	i	o	n

2 ✏️ Match. Write the words.

o	ocean	old
b		
m		
s		
sh		
tr		

cean   ld
eautiful   irt
ountain   un
and   each
ell   ees
ain   ouse

3 🔍✏️ **Look at the picture and answer the questions.**

1) How many people are there? _____ *There are four people.* _____
2) What's the man drinking? _____
3) What's the woman doing? _____
4) Is the dog walking? _____
5) Where's the boy swimming? _____
6) What's the girl picking up? _____
7) How many birds are there? _____
8) What are the birds doing? _____

4 🔍✏️ **Look at the letters and write the words.**

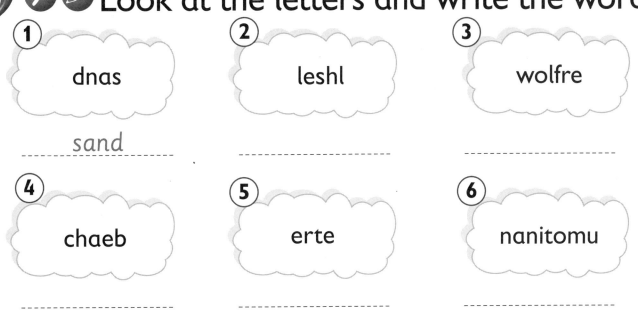

1) dnas

_____ *sand* _____

2) leshl

_____

3) wolfre

_____

4) chaeb

_____

5) erte

_____

6) nanitomu

_____

5 ▶ CD4 🖊 Listen and check (✓) the box.

1) What does Nick want to do?
   a ☐ b ✓ c ☐

2) What does Mary want to have for lunch?
   a ☐ b ☐ c ☐

3) What does Peter want for his birthday?
   a ☐ b ☐ c ☐

4) What does Susan want to drink?
   a ☐ b ☐ c ☐

5) What does Stacey want to play?
   a ☐ b ☐ c ☐

6) Where does John want to go?
   a ☐ b ☐ c ☐

6 🔍 🖊 Read. Write "Yes, he does" or "No, he doesn't."

> **Daniel's birthday list**
> A new bike   A big kite
> A gray robot   A long ruler
> A small camera   A chocolate cake

1) Does Daniel want a new bike? <u>Yes, he does.</u>

2) Does Daniel want a short ruler? _____

3) Does Daniel want a small kite? _____

4) Does Daniel want a gray robot? _____

5) Does Daniel want a small camera? _____

6) Does Daniel want some chocolate ice cream? _____

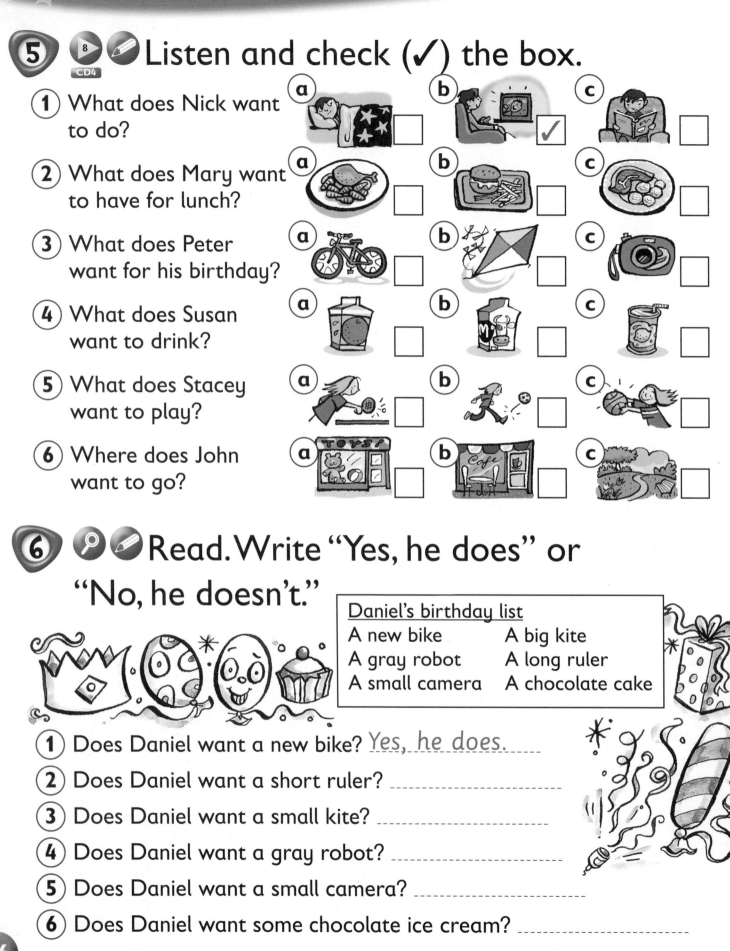

7 Listen and color. There is one example.

8 🔊13 CD4 ✏️ Listen and match.

1. Sam catches his ...   fish.
2. Ben gets ...   stops
3. Jill swims with the ...   hat.
4. Tom ... the dog.   sun.
5. Justine runs in the ...   shells.

a _2_   **b** _____   **c** _____   **d** _____   **e** _____

9 ✏️ Complete the questions. Then answer.

| ugly   new   short   ~~small~~   dirty |

1. Is your kitchen big or _____ small _____ ?

   _____

2. Is your city beautiful or _____ ?

   _____

3. Is your street long or _____ ?

   _____

4. Is your bedroom clean or _____ ?

   _____

5. Is your school old or _____ ?

   _____

10 🔍 ✏️ Complete the words. Stick.

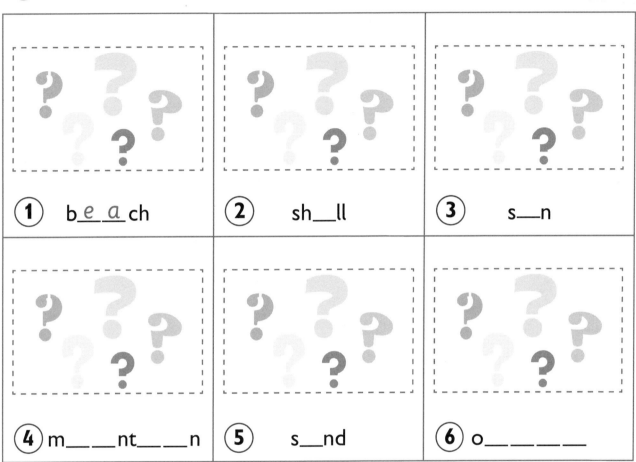

① b_e_ _a_ ch

② sh__ll

③ s__n

④ m__ __nt__ __n

⑤ s__nd

⑥ o__ __ __ __ __

My progress

Check (✓) or put an ✗.

I can talk about my vacation. ☐

I can talk about what I want. ☐

Marie's geography   Maps

Now you! **1** 🔍 ✏️ Read, draw, and color.

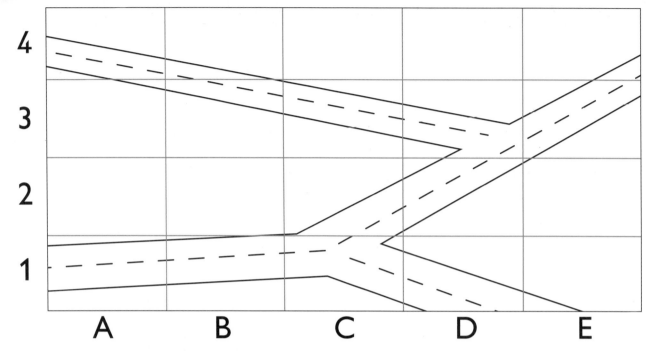

Draw a car in one square. Color it blue.

Draw a tree in one square. Color it brown and green.

Draw a flower in one square. Color it purple and green.

Draw a house in one square. Color it red.

Draw a mountain in one square. Color it gray.

2 💬 ✏️ Ask and answer. Draw.

Where is the car?

D4.

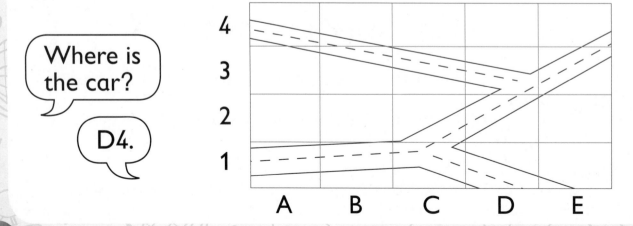

3 18 CD4 🖊 Listen and write the number.

 1

4 🔍🖊 Write and draw.

Me!

1 20 CD4 Listen and connect the dots.

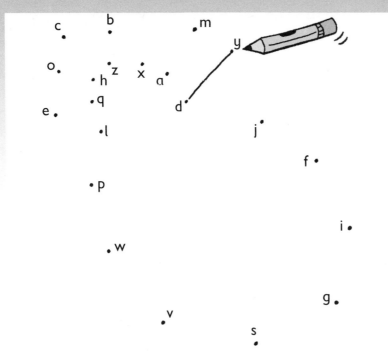

What's this? It's a _____ .

2 21 CD4 Listen and color.

3 🔍✏️ Match the questions and answers.

1. How many sausages do you have? | f | a. He's cooking.

2. Where are they playing badminton? | | b. On the beach.

3. Who's that? | | c. The long, red one.

4. What color's your shirt? | | d. It's green.

5. What's Mr. Star doing? | | e. She's my cousin.

6. Which dress is yours? | | f. I have two.

4 🔍✏️ Read and complete.

eat

→ 10

Grammar reference

1 Order the words.

1 (Tom.) (What's) (his) (He's) (name?)

--------------------------- ? ---------------------------

2 (Who's) (She's) (Mrs.) (Brown.) (my) (teacher,) (she?)

--------------------------- ? ---------------------------

2 Look and write.

Yes, there is.   Yes, there are.   No, there aren't.

1 Is there a whiteboard on the wall? ✓ _____
2 Are there three computers in the classroom? ✗ _____
3 Are there a lot of chairs in the classroom? ✓ _____

3 Circle the question and the answer.

Whoserobotisthis?It'sRobert's.

4 Match the questions and answers.

1 Whose red dress is that?   Yes, they are.
2 Whose blue pants are those?   It's mine.
3 Are those blue socks yours?   They're Dad's.

5 Look and complete.

| 'm not | 'm | 're | 're not | 's | 's not |

① ✓ I _ _ _ _ _ _ _ _ singing.　④ ✗ He _ _ _ _ _ _ _ _ running.

② ✗ I _ _ _ _ _ _ _ _ dancing.　⑤ ✓ She _ _ _ _ _ _ _ _ playing tennis.

③ ✓ You _ _ _ _ _ _ _ _ reading.　⑥ ✗ We _ _ _ _ _ _ _ _ painting.

6 Circle the question and the answer.

Canlhavesomefish,please?Hereyouare.

7 Look and write.

| So do I.　I don't.　So do I. |

① I like rabbits.　☺ _

② I like horses.　☺ _

③ I like spiders.　☹ _

8 Look and complete.

① Where's the café?　It's **bhnide** _ _ _ _ _ _ _ _ the school.

② Where's the park?　It's **ni ofrnt fo** _ _ _ _ _ _ _ _ the hospital.

③ Where's the store?　It's **teewenb** _ _ _ _ _ _ _ _ the park and the apartments.

9 **Write the answers.**

| don't. does. doesn't. do. |

① Do you have a camera?   ✓ Yes, I _ _ _ _ _ _ _ _ _
② Does he have red shoes?   ✗ No, he _ _ _ _ _ _ _ _
③ Does she have a blue bag?   ✓ Yes, she _ _ _ _ _ _ _ _
④ Do you have gray pants?   ✗ No, I _ _ _ _ _ _ _ _

10 **Look and complete.**

| love   don't like   likes   doesn't like |

① ♥ ♥ I _ _ _ _ _ _ _ _ _ _ _ _ _ _ _ _ _ reading.
② ♥   He _ _ _ _ _ _ _ _ _ _ _ _ _ _ _ playing badminton.
③ ✖   She _ _ _ _ _ _ _ _ _ _ _ _ _ _ singing.
④ ✖   I _ _ _ _ _ _ _ _ _ _ _ _ _ _ _ cooking.

11 **Look and complete.**

| No, thank you.   Yes, please. |

① Would you like some chicken?   ✓ _ _ _ _ _ _ _ _ _ _ _ _ _ _
② Would you like some milk?   ✗ _ _ _ _ _ _ _ _ _ _ _ _ _ _

12 **Look and complete.**

| I want to   I don't want to |

① ☺ _ _ _ _ _ _ _ _ _ _ _ _ _ _ go to the beach.
② ☹ _ _ _ _ _ _ _ _ _ _ _ _ _ _ go to a big city.

About me

School: _____

Grade: _____

Teacher: _____

First language(s): _____

Other language(s): _____

Write your favorite words in different languages.

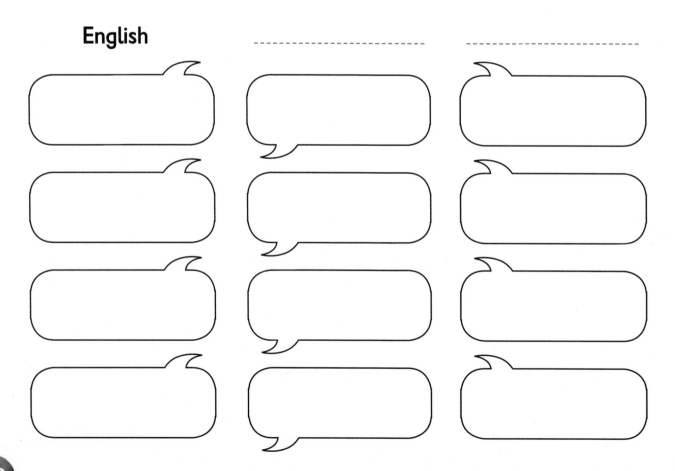

English _____ _____

My language skills

1 Draw the pictures in the spaces below.

  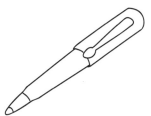 

Listening		:)
Reading		:)
Speaking	(lips)	:)
Writing		:)

2 Do you like doing these things in English?
   Color the faces. Blue = It's good. Green = It's OK.

I can ...   # Units 1-3

1 Listen and color.

11   12   13   14   15

16   17   18   19   20

1

2 💬 How do you spell …?

2

3 🔍 Read and match.

camera   bike   truck   robot   computer game   kite

3

4 ✏️ Write.

My favorite toys are _____

_____ .

4

I can ...

Units 4-6

1 Listen and point.

1
😊

2 💬 Tell your partner about your family.

My family is small. I have ...

2
😊

3 🔍 Read and match.

bread   water   juice   fries   chicken   rice   egg   milk

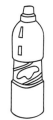   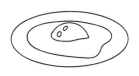

3
😊

4 ✏️ Write about your favorite lunch.

4
😊

I can ...   # Units 7-9

Color the face: I can do it!

1  Listen and point.

2 Point and say.

Use "in," "on," "next to," "under," and "between."

3 Look at the picture. Check (✓) or cross (✗) the boxes.

1   The park is between the toy store and the café. [✗]
2   There's a doll and a car in the toy store. [ ]
3   There's a street and there's a park. [ ]
4   The monkey is under the tree. [ ]
5   There's a hospital next to the café. [ ]
6   The ball is on the table. [ ]

4 Write about your favorite clothes.

1

2

3

4

I can... Units 10-12

1 🎧 Listen. Say "yes" or "no."

1 😊

2 💬 Point and say.

2 😊

3 🔍 Read and circle the pictures above.

What would Ben like?

I'd like some lemonade and a sausage. Oh, and I'd like some watermelon, please!

3 😊

4 ✏️ Write.

I can see _____

and _____ in the mountains.

I can see _____

and _____ at the beach.

4 😊

English and me

I learn English ...

... in school ☑

... at home (private classes) ☐

... at an academy ☐

... in the summer ☐

My favorite English activities are:

listening ☐ reading ☐ speaking ☐ writing ☐

games ☐ songs ☐ using the book ☐

I speak English to my _____ .

An English song I like: _____

An English book I like: _____

An English movie I like: _____

People speak English in _____ .
I want to go there on vacation!

My school bag

Draw your school bag. What's inside it?
Color your picture.

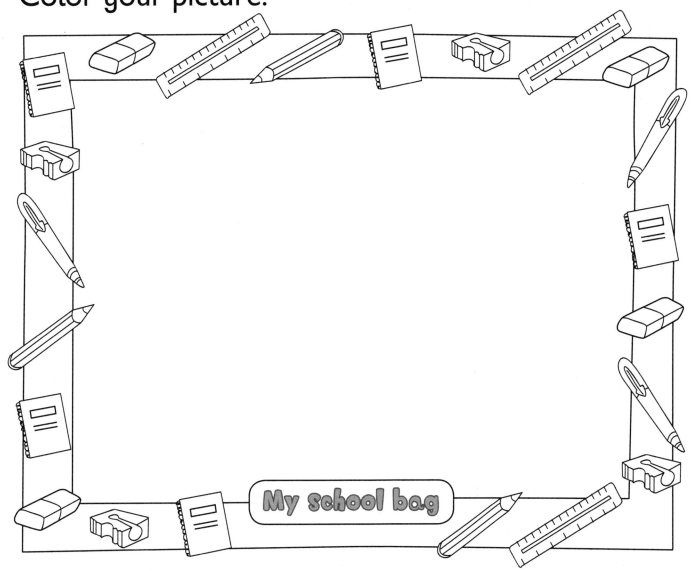

My school bag

Now write about your school bag.

My bedroom

Draw or stick a picture of your bedroom.

My bedroom

Do you have these things in your bedroom?
Write "yes" or "no."

phone _____   mirror _____   armchair _____   guitar _____

bookcase _____   computer _____   cupboard _____   toys _____

lamp _____   rug _____   clock _____   window _____

What do you have in your bedroom?

_____

My family

Draw or stick a picture of you and your family.

My family

The people in my picture are:

How old are they?

My ------------------------------ is ------------- years old.

My ------------------------------ is ------------- years old.

Things I love

Draw or stick pictures of things you love.

I love ...

My favorite food is _____ .

My favorite sport is _____ .

My favorite animal is _____ .

My favorite _____ is _____ .

I love _____ !

My favorite clothes

Draw or stick pictures of your favourite clothes.

My favorite T-shirt.　My favorite shoes.

My favorite _____ .

A vacation

Draw or stick a picture from your vacation.

My vacation

What people, things, and places are in your picture?

Write about your vacation.

Thanks and Acknowledgments

Authors' thanks

Many thanks to everyone at Cambridge University Press and in particular to:

Rosemary Bradley for supervising the whole project and for her keen editorial eye;
Emily Hird for her energy, enthusiasm, and enormous organisational capacity;
Colin Sage for his good ideas and helpful suggestions;
Claire Appleyard for her editorial contribution.

Many thanks to Karen Elliot for her expertise and enthusiasm in the writing of the Phonics sections.

We would also like to thank all our pupils and colleagues at Star English, El Palmar, Murcia, and especially Jim Kelly and Julie Woodman for their help and suggestions at various stages of the project.

Dedications

I would like to dedicate this book to the women who have been my pillars of strength: Milagros Marín, Sara de Alba, Elia Navarro, and Maricarmen Balsalobre - CN

To Paloma, for her love, encouragement, and unwavering support. Thanks. - MT

The Authors and Publishers would like to thank the following teachers for their help in reviewing the material and for the invaluable feedback they provided:

Alice Matovich, Cecilia Sanchez, Florencia Durante, Maria Loe Antigona, Argentina; Erica Santos, Brazil; Ma Xin, Ren Xiaochi, China; Albeiro Monsalve Marin, Colombia; Agata Jankiewicz, Poland; Maria Antonia Castro, Spain; Catherine Taylor, Turkey.

The authors and publishers would like to thank the following consultants for their invaluable feedback:

Coralyn Bradshaw, Pippa Mayfield, Hilary Ratcliff, Melanie Williams.

We would also like to thank all the teachers who allowed us to observe their classes and who gave up their invaluable time for interviews and focus groups.

The authors and publishers are grateful to the following illustrators:

Andrew Hennessey; Beatrice Costamagna, c/o Pickled ink; Chris Garbutt, c/o Arena; Emily Skinner, c/o Graham-Cameron Illustration; Gary Swift; James Elston, c/o Sylvie Poggio; Kelly Kennedy, c/o Syvlie Poggio; Lisa Smith; Lisa Williams, c/o Sylvie Poggio; Marie Simpson, c/o Pickled ink; Matt Ward, c/o Beehive; Melanie Sharp, c/o Syvlie Poggio.

The authors and publishers acknowledge the following sources of copyright material and are grateful for the permissions granted. While every effort has been made, it has not always been possible to identify the sources of all the material used or to trace all copyright holders. If any omissions are brought to our notice, we will be happy to include the appropriate acknowledgments on reprinting.

p.17 (background): Thinkstock; p.31 (background): Thinkstock; p.45 (background): Thinkstock; p.60 (sheep): Shutterstock/chaoss; p.60 (bird): Shutterstock/Kutlayev Dmitry; p.60 (frog): Shutterstock/Alfredo Maiquez; p.60 (elephant): Shutterstock/Johan Swanepoel; p.60 (cow): Shutterstock/Martin Nemec; p.60 (cat): Shutterstock/elwynn; p.61(background): Thinkstock; p.77 (background): Thinkstock; p.91 (background): Thinkstock.

Commissioned photography on page 60 by Trevor Clifford Photography.

The publishers are grateful to the following contributors:

Louise Edgeworth: picture research and art direction
Wild Apple Design Ltd: page design
Blooberry: additional design
Lon Chan: cover design
John Green and Tim Woolf, TEFL Audio: audio recordings
John Marshall Media, Inc. and Lisa Hutchins: audio recordings for the American English edition
Robert Lee: song writing
hyphen S.A.: publishing management, American English edition

Hi again! (page 9)

black   purple   yellow

green   pink   blue

 # Back to school (page 15)

 # Play time! (page 23)

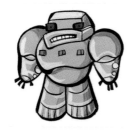